Wordless Workshop™

Wordless Workshop™

120 of the Best, Easy-to-Make
Projects from Roy Doty's
Monthly Feature in

Popular science

DAVID & CHARLES
Newton Abbot   London

Roy Doty's *Wordless Workshop* reprinted from *Popular Science* with permission © 1971, 1972, 1973, 1974, 1975, 1976, 1977, 1978, 1979, 1980, 1981, 1982, 1983, 1984, 1985 Times Mirror Magazines, Inc.

British Library Cataloguing in Publication Data

Doty, Roy
  Wordless workshop: 120 of the best, easy-to-make projects from Roy Doty's monthly feature in popular science.
    1. Dwellings—Maintenance and repair—Amateurs' manuals 2. Dwellings—Remodeling—Amateurs' manuals
    I. Title II. Popular science monthly
643'.7   TH4817.3
ISBN 0-7153-9080-5

First published in Great Britain by David & Charles 1987

Printed in the United States of America
for David & Charles Publishers plc
Brunel House
Newton Abbot Devon

CONTENTS

A Word from the Creator of *Wordless Workshop*

More than thirty years ago, I approached the editors of *Popular Science* with the idea of a feature page illustrating innovative solutions to common household problems. There would be no measurements, no specifications, and no words. The editors agreed to give the idea a try, and *Wordless Workshop* has been a monthly feature in the magazine ever since.

For the first few years, I developed the projects to be illustrated, but soon readers began to write to the magazine offering their own suggestions. Their creativity has been expressed in almost every possible medium—written descriptions, simple drawings, photographs, complete constructions in large packages, and lately in words and pictures produced on home computers. Nowadays, several hundred letters arrive at *Popular Science* every week. I have heard from residents of every state in the Union and dozens of countries around the world, men and women, boys and girls, ages 8 to 82. I have heard from the children of some of the earliest contributors to *Wordless*, and I look forward to hearing from their grandchildren.

Those correspondents whose ideas have been incorporated in this book are acknowledged on page 127, and I would like to add my personal thanks to them and to the thousands of others who continue to provide inspiration for *Wordless Workshop.*

—Roy Doty

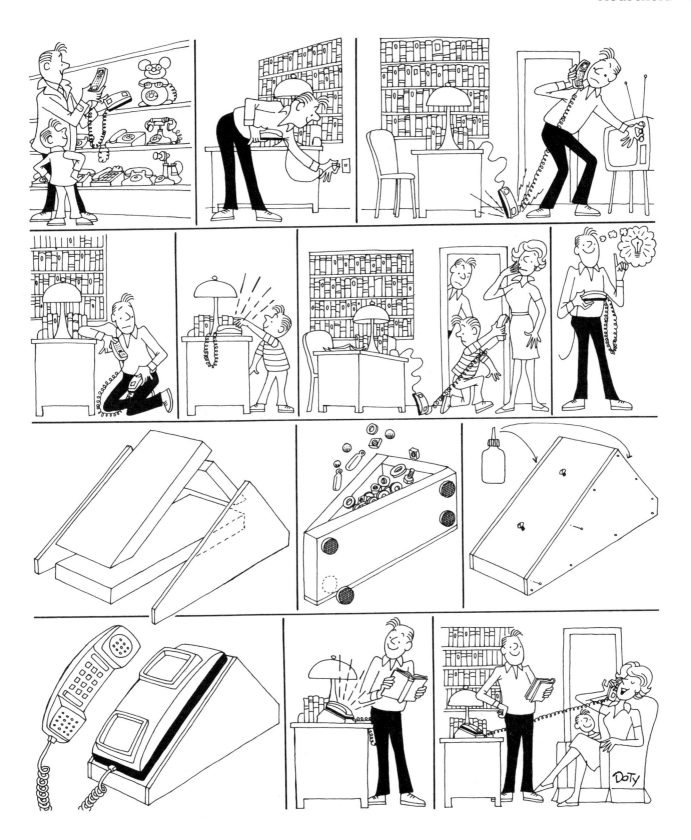

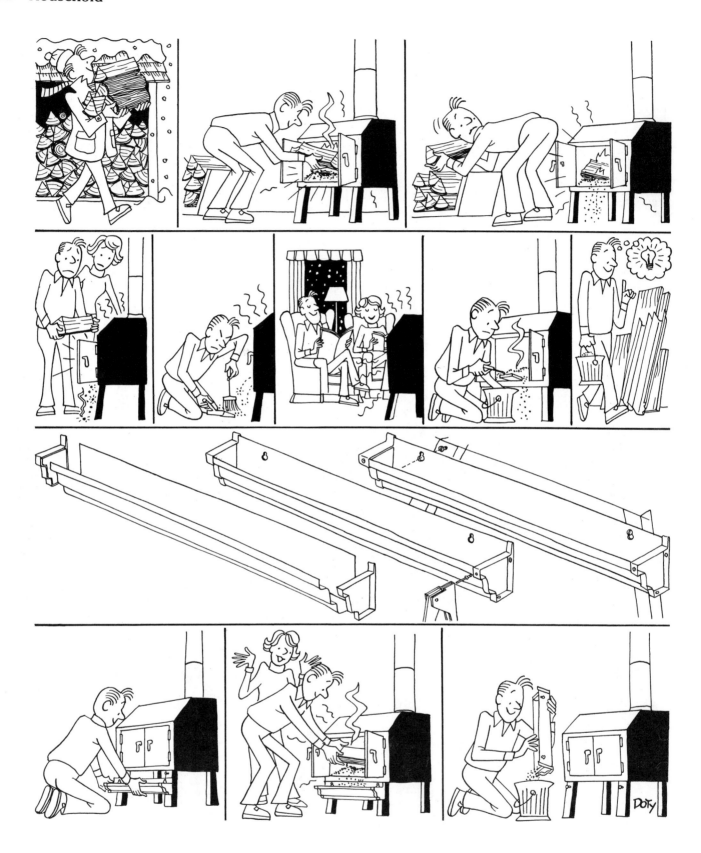

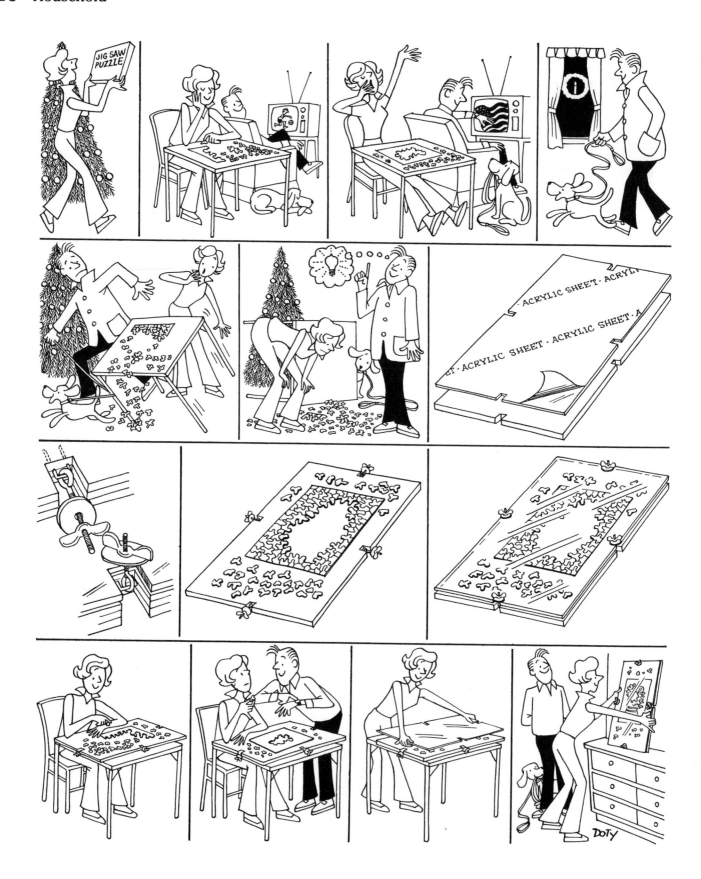

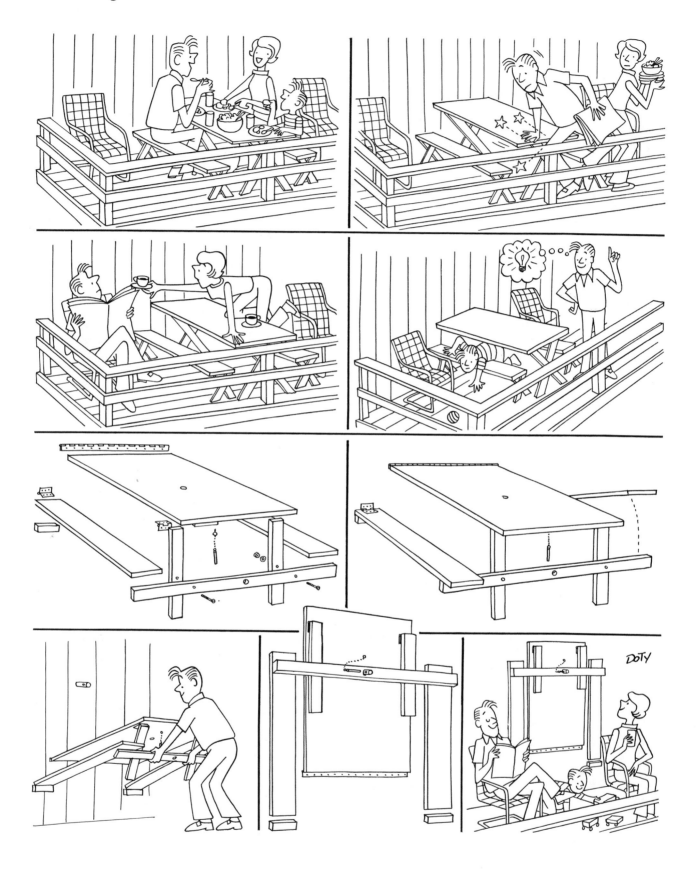

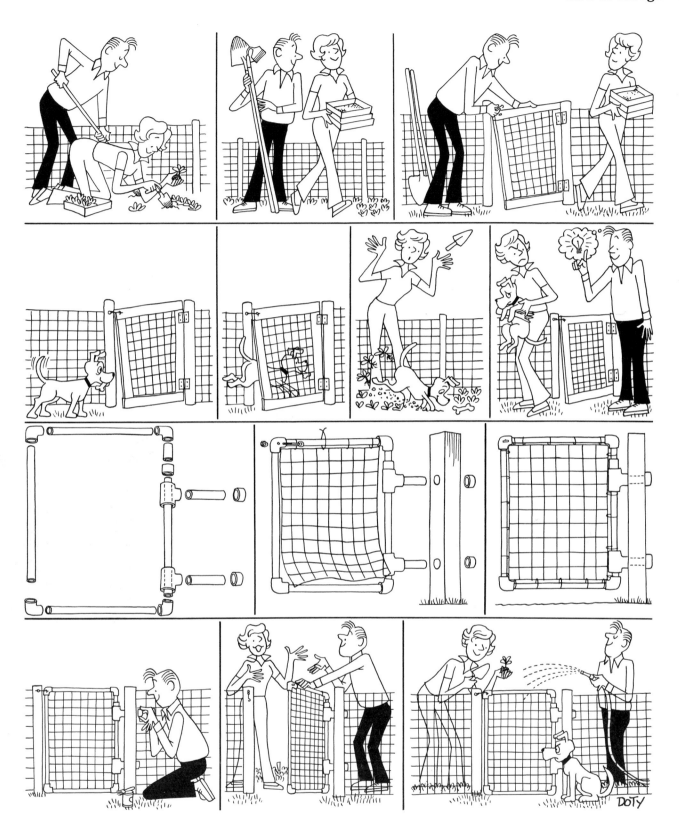

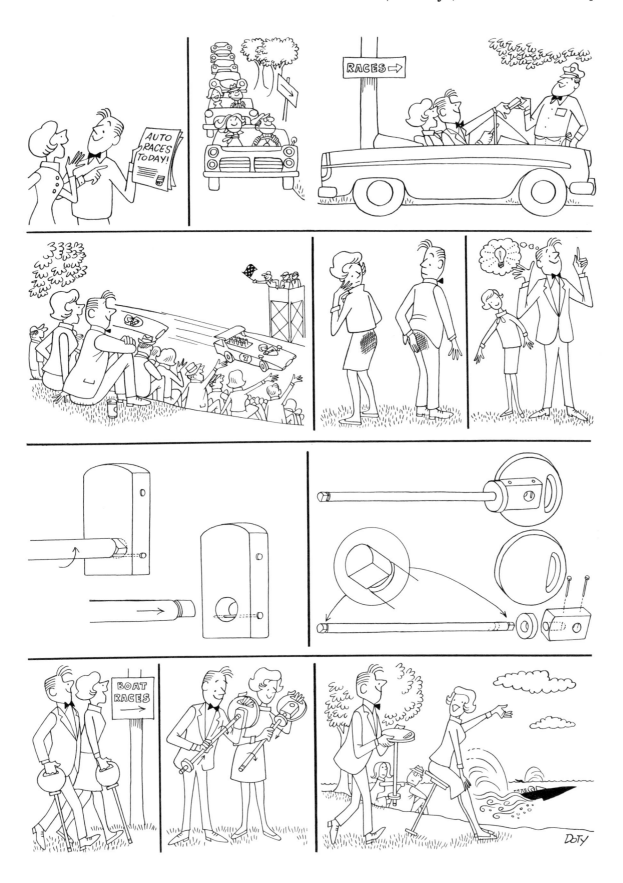

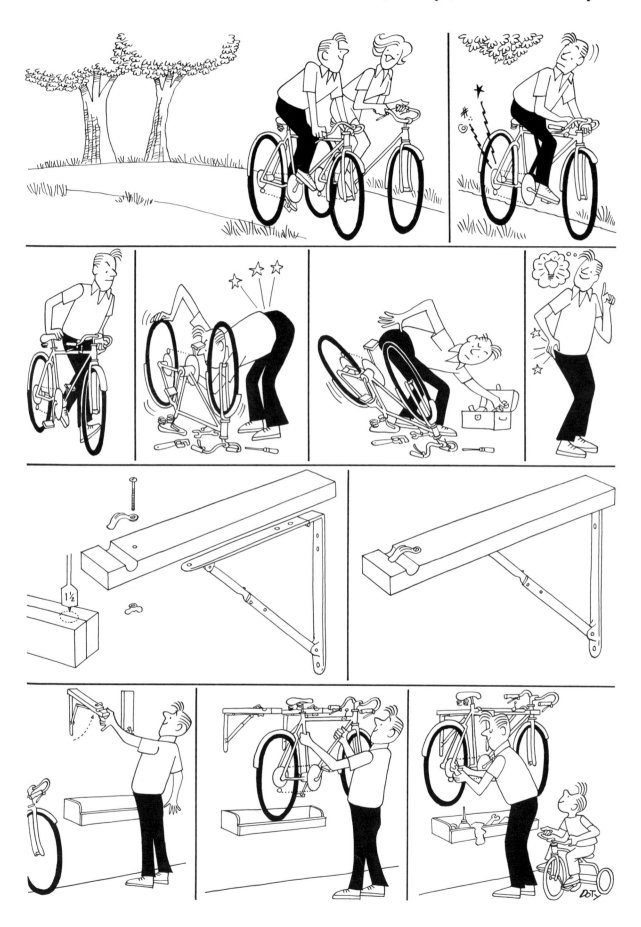

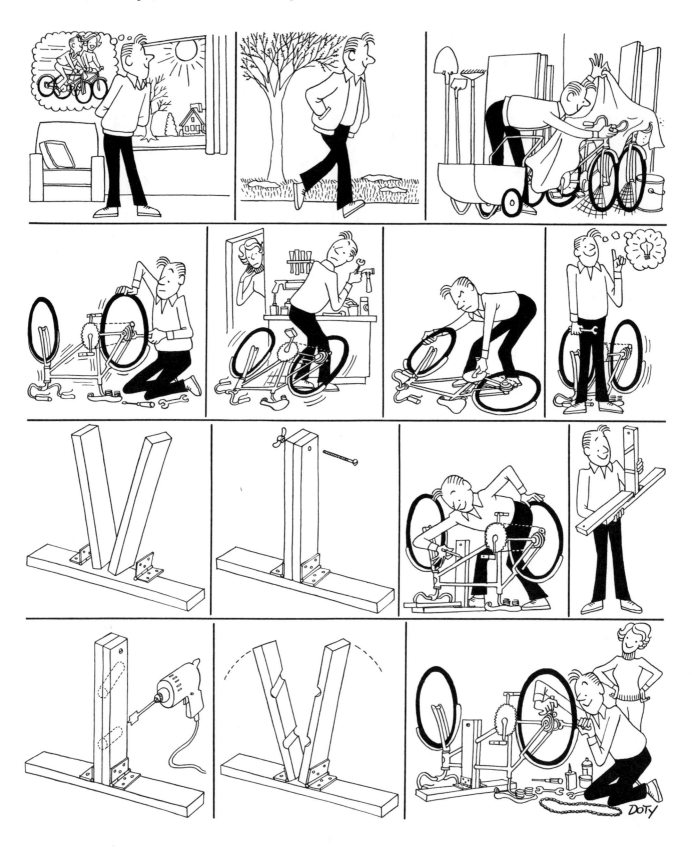

The author is grateful to the following people for their ideas:

Nickolas J. Aiuto, Harry Amos, Dennis Badal, Michael J. Bain, Laurent Beaucage, Charles G. Bieber, Gustave Blabas, Gary Borlaug, W. Paul Brandt, Lorraine Brendzy, Carolyn Brooks, D. S. Burch, Mack D. Calhoun, John Christian, Roger E. D'Anna, William K. Daulley, David Dowless, J. Howard Dunn, Myron Eppley, Terry Falk, Albert Fiebig, Frank Flickinger, James Garrie, Edwin Gerson, Joseph Guess, Anthony Gingo, Barry Glunts, Ottmar Goebel, Gordon Gullikson, Bob Hall, Allen Hancock, David E. Harper, Kristen Hawkins, Clyde Heeler, T. L. Henley, L. H. Hinrichsen, Donald Hoger, Kurt S. Hollenbeck, John Janiec, John C. Johnson, T. K. Joynt, Ted Kaiser, Richard Keith, Alex Koval, Henry E. Kruszynsky, Sidney Lederman, D. B. Lewis, Mark Lindsay, Doug Livingston, Terri McBride, H. W. McGaughey, John McNeill, Bob Mellin, Terry Mitchell, E. W. Moorman, Gus Mueller, Gary Nelson, John L. O'Connell, Joe Patzer, Vernon L. Paul, Bruce D. Philpott, W. C. Pickard, L. M. Powell, Ronald E. Proulx, Ed Quigley, Russell Z. Railsback, Lenn Richter, Rex Rickley, Pat Rorden, Marty Rosen, Jeff N. Schmidt, Fred Schweitzer, Chuck Sekera, Jerry E. Shepherd, Raymond Singer, Robert O. Snyder, Doris Squire, R. H. Stein, Sal Stella, Walter Stumpf, Harrison Syler, Frank Tassone, D. C. Taylor, W. G. Taylor, George Tenselshof, James Tira, Dan Tucker, Arthur Van Gilder, Kirk Vredevelt, Keith Wagoner, Wilson Walters, Sally A. Ward, David Watson, John Weitendorf, Tom Wetmiller, David Williams, V. M. Wilson, J. Wlodarczyk, Edmund Woo, John Y. Yoon, John Zirngibl.

Popular Science magazine awards $50 for the ideas it selects to appear in *Wordless Workshop*. If you have an idea (no diagram necessary) send it and your Social Security number to:

Wordless
Popular Science
380 Madison Avenue
New York, New York 10017

Only purchased ideas can be acknowledged.

To order more copies of Roy Doty's *Wordless Workshop*, use the coupon below, or call toll-free (800) 221-7945. In New York, call (212) 674-5151.

....

Please send me_____copy(ies) of *Wordless Workshop* by Roy Doty @ $6.95 each plus $1.50 postage and handling for the first book and 50¢ per copy for each additional book.

I enclose a check or money order for $ _____.

_____
NAME

_____
ADDRESS

_____
CITY   STATE   ZIP

Return coupon with check to:

St. Martin's Press, Inc.
Cash Sales Department
175 Fifth Avenue
New York, NY 10010